# THE JPS B'NAI MITZVAH TORAH COMMENTARY

**Va-yetse'** (Genesis 28:10–32:3)
Haftarah (Hosea 12:13–14:10)

Rabbi Jeffrey K. Salkin

The Jewish Publication Society · Philadelphia
University of Nebraska Press · Lincoln

# INTRODUCTION

News flash: the most important thing about becoming bar or bat mitzvah isn't the party. Nor is it the presents. Nor even being able to celebrate with your family and friends—as wonderful as those things are. Nor is it even standing before the congregation and reading the prayers of the liturgy—as important as that is.

No, the most important thing about becoming bar or bat mitzvah is sharing Torah with the congregation. And why is that? Because of all Jewish skills, that is the most important one.

Here is what is true about rites of passage: you can tell what a culture values by the tasks it asks its young people to perform on their way to maturity. In American culture, you become responsible for driving, responsible for voting, and yes, responsible for drinking responsibly.

In some cultures, the rite of passage toward maturity includes some kind of trial, or a test of strength. Sometimes, it is a kind of "outward bound" camping adventure. Among the Maasai tribe in Africa, it is traditional for a young person to hunt and kill a lion. In some Hispanic cultures, fifteen year-old girls celebrate the *quinceañera*, which marks their entrance into maturity.

What is Judaism's way of marking maturity? It combines both of these rites of passage: *responsibility* and *test*. You show that you are on your way to becoming a *responsible* Jewish adult through a public *test* of strength and knowledge—reading or chanting Torah, and then teaching it to the congregation.

This is the most important Jewish ritual mitzvah (commandment), and that is how you demonstrate that you are, truly, bar or bat mitzvah—old enough to be responsible for the mitzvot.

## What Is Torah?

So, what exactly is the Torah? You probably know this already, but let's review.

The Torah (teaching) consists of "the five books of Moses," sometimes also called the *chumash* (from the Hebrew word *chameish,* which means "five"), or, sometimes, the Greek word Pentateuch (which means "the five teachings").

Here are the five books of the Torah, with their common names and their Hebrew names.

> **Genesis (The beginning), which in Hebrew is Bere'shit (from the first words—"When God began to create").** Bere'shit spans the years from Creation to Joseph's death in Egypt. Many of the Bible's best stories are in Genesis: the creation story itself; Adam and Eve in the Garden of Eden; Cain and Abel; Noah and the Flood; and the tales of the Patriarchs and Matriarchs, Abraham, Isaac, Jacob, Sarah, Rebekah, Rachel, and Leah. It also includes one of the greatest pieces of world literature, the story of Joseph, which is actually the oldest complete novel in history, comprising more than one-quarter of all Genesis.

> **Exodus (Getting out), which in Hebrew is Shemot (These are the names).** Exodus begins with the story of the Israelite slavery in Egypt. It then moves to the rise of Moses as a leader, and the Israelites' liberation from slavery. After the Israelites leave Egypt, they experience the miracle of the parting of the Sea of Reeds (or "Red Sea"); the giving of the Ten Commandments at Mount Sinai; the idolatry of the Golden Calf; and the design and construction of the Tabernacle and of the ark for the original tablets of the law, which our ancestors carried with them in the desert. Exodus also includes various ethical and civil laws, such as "You shall not wrong a stranger or oppress him, for you were strangers in the land of Egypt" (22:20).

> **Leviticus (about the Levites), or, in Hebrew, Va-yikra' (And God called).** It goes into great detail about the kinds of sacrifices that the ancient Israelites brought as offerings; the laws of ritual purity; the animals that were permitted and forbidden for eating (the beginnings of the tradition of kashrut, the Jewish dietary laws); the diagnosis of various skin diseases; the ethical laws of holiness; the ritual calendar of the Jewish year; and various agricultural laws concerning the treatment of the Land of Israel. Leviticus is basically the manual of ancient Judaism.

> Numbers (because the book begins with the census of the Isra-
> elites), or, in Hebrew, Be-midbar (In the wilderness). The book
> describes the forty years of wandering in the wilderness and the
> various rebellions against Moses. The constant theme: "Egypt
> wasn't so bad. Maybe we should go back." The greatest rebellion
> against Moses was the negative reports of the spies about the
> Land of Israel, which discouraged the Israelites from wanting to
> move forward into the land. For that reason, the "wilderness gen-
> eration" must die off before a new generation can come into ma-
> turity and finish the journey.

> Deuteronomy (The repetition of the laws of the Torah), or, in
> Hebrew, Devarim (The words). The final book of the Torah is,
> essentially, Moses's farewell address to the Israelites as they pre-
> pare to enter the Land of Israel. Here we find various laws that
> had been previously taught, though sometimes with different
> wording. Much of Deuteronomy contains laws that will be im-
> portant to the Israelites as they enter the Land of Israel—laws
> concerning the establishment of a monarchy and the ethics of
> warfare. Perhaps the most famous passage from Deuteronomy
> contains the *Shema,* the declaration of God's unity and unique-
> ness, and the *Ve-ahavta,* which follows it. Deuteronomy ends with
> the death of Moses on Mount Nebo as he looks across the Jordan
> Valley into the land that he will not enter.

Jews read the Torah in sequence—starting with Bere'shit right after Simchat Torah in the autumn, and then finishing Devarim on the
following Simchat Torah. Each Torah portion is called a parashah (division; sometimes called a *sidrah,* a place in the order of the Torah
reading). The stories go around in a full circle, reminding us that we
can always gain more insights and more wisdom from the Torah. This
means that if you don't "get" the meaning this year, don't worry—it
will come around again.

### And What Else? The Haftarah

We read or chant the Torah from the Torah scroll—the most sacred
thing that a Jewish community has in its possession. The Torah is

written without vowels, and the ability to read it and chant it is part of the challenge and the test.

But there is more to the synagogue reading. Every Torah reading has an accompanying haftarah reading. Haftarah means "conclusion," because there was once a time when the service actually ended with that reading. Some scholars believe that the reading of the haftarah originated at a time when non-Jewish authorities outlawed the reading of the Torah, and the Jews read the haftarah sections instead. In fact, in some synagogues, young people who become bar or bat mitzvah read very little Torah and instead read the entire haftarah portion.

The haftarah portion comes from the Nevi'im, the prophetic books, which are the second part of the Jewish Bible. It is either read or chanted from a Hebrew Bible, or maybe from a booklet or a photocopy.

The ancient sages chose the haftarah passages because their themes reminded them of the words or stories in the Torah text. Sometimes, they chose *haftarah* with special themes in honor of a festival or an upcoming festival.

Not all books in the prophetic section of the Hebrew Bible consist of prophecy. Several are historical. For example:

The book of Joshua tells the story of the conquest and settlement of Israel.

The book of Judges speaks of the period of early tribal rulers who would rise to power, usually for the purpose of uniting the tribes in war against their enemies. Some of these leaders are famous: Deborah, the great prophetess and military leader, and Samson, the biblical strong man.

The books of Samuel start with Samuel, the last judge, and then move to the creation of the Israelite monarchy under Saul and David (approximately 1000 BCE).

The books of Kings tell of the death of King David, the rise of King Solomon, and how the Israelite kingdom split into the Northern Kingdom of Israel and the Southern Kingdom of Judah (approximately 900 BCE).

And then there are the books of the prophets, those spokesmen for God whose words fired the Jewish conscience. Their names are immortal: Isaiah, Jeremiah, Ezekiel, Amos, Hosea, among others.

Someone once said: "There is no evidence of a biblical prophet ever being invited back a second time for dinner." Why? Because the prophets were tough. They had no patience for injustice, apathy, or hypocrisy. No one escaped their criticisms. Here's what they taught:

› God commands the Jews to behave decently toward one another. In fact, God cares more about basic ethics and decency than about ritual behavior.
› God chose the Jews *not* for special privileges, but for special duties to humanity.
› As bad as the Jews sometimes were, there was always the possibility that they would improve their behavior.
› As bad as things might be now, it will not always be that way. Someday, there will be universal justice and peace. Human history is moving forward toward an ultimate conclusion that some call the Messianic Age: a time of universal peace and prosperity for the Jewish people and for all the people of the world.

## Your Mission—To Teach Torah to the Congregation

On the day when you become bar or bat mitzvah, you will be reading, or chanting, Torah—in Hebrew. You will be reading, or chanting, the haftarah—in Hebrew. That is the major skill that publicly marks the becoming of bar or bat mitzvah. But, perhaps even more important than that, you need to be able to teach something about the Torah portion, and perhaps the haftarah as well.

And that is where this book comes in. It will be a very valuable resource for you, and your family, in the b'nai mitzvah process.

Here is what you will find in it:

› A brief **summary** of every Torah portion. This is a basic overview of the portion; and, while it might not refer to everything in the Torah portion, it will explain its most important aspects.
› A list of the **major ideas** in the Torah portion. The purpose: to make the Torah portion real, in ways that we can relate to. Every Torah portion contains unique ideas, and when you put all

of those ideas together, you actually come up with a list of Judaism's most important ideas.

› Two **divrei Torah** ("words of Torah," or "sermonettes") for each portion. These *divrei Torah* explain significant aspects of the Torah portion in accessible, reader-friendly language. Each *devar Torah* contains references to **traditional** Jewish sources (those that were written before the modern era), as well as **modern** sources and quotes. We have searched, far and wide, to find sources that are unusual, interesting, and not just the "same old stuff" that many people already know about the Torah portion. Why did we include these minisermons in the volume? Not because we want you to simply copy those sermons and pass them off as your own (that would be cheating), though you are free to quote from them. We included them so that you can see what is possible— how you can try to make meaning for yourself out of the words of Torah.

› **Connections:** This is perhaps the most valuable part. It's a list of questions that you can ask yourself, or that others might help you think about—any of which can lead to the creation of your *devar Torah.*

Note: you don't have to like everything that's in a particular Torah portion. Some aren't that loveable. Some are hard to understand; some are about religious practices that people today might find confusing, and even offensive; some contain ideas that we might find totally outmoded.

But this doesn't have to get in the way. After all, most kids spend a lot of time thinking about stories that contain ideas that modern people would find totally bizarre. Any good medieval fantasy story falls into that category.

And we also believe that, if you spend just a little bit of time with those texts, you can begin to understand what the author was trying to say.

This volume goes one step further. Sometimes, the haftarah comes off as a second thought, and no one really thinks about it. We have tried to solve that problem by including a **summary** of each haftarah, and then a mini-sermon on the haftarah. This will help you learn how these sacred words are relevant to today's world, and even to your own life.

All Bible quotations come from the NJPS translation, which is found in the many different editions of the JPS TANAKH; in the Conservative movement's *Etz Hayim: Torah and Commentary;* in the Reform movement's *Torah: A Modern Commentary;* and in other Bible commentaries and study guides.

### How Do I Write a *Devar Torah?*

It really is easier than it looks.

There are many ways of thinking about the *devar Torah.* It is, of course, a short sermon on the meaning of the Torah (and, perhaps, the haftarah) portion. It might even be helpful to think of the *devar Torah* as a "book report" on the portion itself.

The most important thing you can know about this sacred task is: *Learn* the words. *Love* the words. Teach people what it could mean to *live* the words.

Here's a basic outline for a *devar Torah:*

"My Torah portion is (name of portion)_____,
    from the book of _____, chapter

    _____.

"In my Torah portion, we learn that_____
    (Summary of portion)

"For me, the most important lesson of this Torah portion is (what is the best thing in the portion? Take the portion as a whole; your *devar Torah* does not have to be only, or specifically, on the verses that you are reading).

"As I learned my Torah portion, I found myself wondering:

> ‣ *Raise a question that the Torah portion itself raises.*
> ‣ *"Pick a fight"* with the portion. Argue with it.
> ‣ *Answer a question* that is listed in the "Connections" section of each Torah portion.
> ‣ *Suggest a question to your rabbi* that you would want the rabbi to answer in his or her own *devar Torah* or sermon.

"I have lived the values of the Torah by _____
(here, you can talk about how the Torah portion relates to your own life. If you have done a mitzvah project, you can talk about that here).

## How To Keep It from Being Boring (and You from Being Bored)

Some people just don't like giving traditional speeches. From our perspective, that's really okay. Perhaps you can teach Torah in a different way—one that makes sense to you.

➤ Write an "open letter" to one of the characters in your Torah portion. "Dear Abraham: I hope that your trip to Canaan was not too hard . . ." "Dear Moses: Were you afraid when you got the Ten Commandments on Mount Sinai? I sure would have been . . ."

➤ Write a news story about what happens. Imagine yourself to be a television or news reporter. "Residents of neighboring cities were horrified yesterday as the wicked cities of Sodom and Gomorrah were burned to the ground. Some say that God was responsible . . ."

➤ Write an imaginary interview with a character in your Torah portion.

➤ Tell the story from the point of view of another character, or a minor character, in the story. For instance, tell the story of the Garden of Eden from the point of view of the serpent. Or the story of the Binding of Isaac from the point of view of the ram, which was substituted for Isaac as a sacrifice. Or perhaps the story of the sale of Joseph from the point of view of his coat, which was stripped off him and dipped in a goat's blood.

➤ Write a poem about your Torah portion.

➤ Write a song about your Torah portion.

➤ Write a play about your Torah portion, and have some friends act it out with you.

➤ Create a piece of artwork about your Torah portion.

The bottom line is: Make this a joyful experience. Yes—it could even be fun.

### The Very Last Thing You Need to Know at This Point

The Torah scroll is written without vowels. Why? Don't *sofrim* (Torah scribes) know the vowels?

Of course they do.

So, why do they leave the vowels out?

One reason is that the Torah came into existence at a time when sages were still arguing about the proper vowels, and the proper pronunciation.

But here is another reason: The Torah text, as we have it today, and as it sits in the scroll, is actually *an unfinished work*. Think of it: the words are just sitting there. Because they have no vowels, it is as if they have no voice.

When we read the Torah publicly, we give voice to the ancient words. And when we find meaning in those ancient words, and we talk about those meanings, those words jump to life. They enter our lives. They make our world deeper and better.

Mazal tov to you, and your family. This is your journey toward Jewish maturity. Love it.

# THE TORAH

### ❖ Va-yetse': Genesis 28:10–32:3

Jacob is not only a little sneaky—disguising himself so that he can steal his father's blessing from Esau. He is also now scared, because Esau has threatened to kill him for doing so. And, so, Jacob runs away—back to his extended family in Haran. On the way, he has a strange dream—of angels ascending and descending a stairway (or ladder). It is one of the most famous dreams in all literature and art (not to mention "Stairway to Heaven" by Led Zeppelin, which might be the most-played song in the history of radio).

When he gets to Haran (or Paddan-aram, or Aram-naharaim—the place has several names), he meets and falls in love with his cousin, Rachel. But Jacob's uncle Laban is no less sneaky than Jacob (in fact, you might say that the extended Abraham family has the "sneaky gene"). He tricks Jacob by switching the older "average-looking" sister, Leah, for the beautiful Rachel. Jacob winds up working seven more years in order to marry Rachel. Rachel, Leah, and their handmaidens, Bilhah and Zilpah, give birth to the children who will ultimately become the ancestors of the tribes of Israel.

## Summary

➤ On his way to Haran, Jacob dreams about a stairway reaching up to the heavens, with angels going up and down. God speaks to Jacob and blesses him and his descendants. (28:10–22)

➤ Jacob meets Rachel and her father, Laban, who is also Jacob's uncle. Jacob falls in love with Rachel, but Laban has other ideas; he wants his older daughter, Leah, to marry first. (29:1–35)

➤ Just as there was a rivalry between Jacob and Esau, there is a rivalry between Rachel, who is childless, and her sister Leah, who has many children. (30:1–24)

➤ Jacob tries an experiment in breeding goats and sheep, with interesting results. (30:25–43)

➤ Jacob and his family flee from Laban. (31:1–54; 32:1–3)

## The Big Ideas

> **Dreams have meaning.** Jews have always been fascinated by dreams and dream interpretation. From ancient times, Jews have sensed that sometimes dreams can reveal a person's destiny. We should pay attention to our dreams; they often have something very important to tell us.

> **The Jews are a wandering people.** Jewish history is the story of Jews moving from place to place—exiled from the Land of Israel, from England, Spain, Germany, Russia, and elsewhere. That is why the story of Jacob is so important. He wanders a lot. He often has to escape from uncomfortable places. Jacob is a model for the Jewish people throughout history.

> **What goes around, comes around.** Just as Jacob deceived his brother and his father, he is deceived by his uncle and father-in-law, Laban. Be careful of what you do—it could come back to haunt you, or, even better, reward you!

> **Jews knows what it's like to be slaves.** Jacob's years of servitude to Laban are a sort of dress rehearsal for what it was like for the Israelites as slaves in Egypt. And the way that Jacob and his family escape from Laban reminds us of the Exodus.

*Divrei Torah*

### WHO WERE THOSE ANGELS, AND WHAT
### WERE THEY DOING ON THE LADDER?

Jacob saw angels in a dream. Assume for a moment that angels exist—symbolically if not literally—as messengers of some kind. The Torah tells us that angels of God were "going up and down on it [the stairway]." If we further assume that angels came from heaven, why did they start by going *up* the stairway?

The first possibility: The angels symbolize Jacob's transition from childhood to entering adulthood. As Rabbi Solomon B. Freehof writes: "The first group of angels were the angels that had accompanied him from home. But a new group of angels was descending to accompany him further on his journey. Jacob is now going on the journey of life, to be self-reliant and an adult." Jacob's dream, therefore, is a rite of passage from childhood to adulthood—an ancient "bar mitzvah!"

The second possibility: The angels represent Jewish history. An ancient tradition says that Jacob saw angels representing every ancient nation that would conquer the Jews—Assyria, Babylon, Persia, Greece, Rome—going up and coming down again. God invited Jacob, as the ancestor of the Jewish people, to climb up the stairway. God was saying to Jacob: dare to become a world empire! But Jacob refused; he didn't want to risk it. He didn't want the Jewish people to simply become an empire like all the other ancient empires. He didn't want the Jews to be famous just for having military power. He knew that the power of the Jews was in words and what words could teach. He was also afraid that if he went up the ladder, someday his descendants would have to come down the ladder—that his people's future success might only be temporary.

The third possibility: The angels represent Jacob himself—a life filled with ups and downs. The ancient Jewish philosopher Philo said: "Life is comparable to a ladder because of its irregular course. A single day can carry the person who is set on high downward, and someone else upward. None of us remains in the same circumstances." It's like the old board game Chutes and Ladders—you never know when you are going to climb up, or fall down.

Life is, indeed, like a ladder. Our job is to learn how to live with those ups and downs, and to make the best of those opportunities for growth.

LIVING WITH LABAN

Sometimes, the way that the text appears in the Torah scroll itself tells its own story. Every other Torah portion, except this one, appears in the Torah with spaces and "paragraphs." Not this one; it's one large, closed block of text. Why?

The layout of the Torah text is like Jacob himself—and then his family—who became "closed up" and basically imprisoned within the household of his uncle and father-in-law, Laban. Jacob first met Rachel and he immediately fell in love with her. He thought that he was marrying Rachel, but on their wedding night, under the cover of darkness, Laban switched her sister, Leah, for Rachel. Jacob loved Rachel so much that he worked another seven years in order to win her hand in marriage too. Laban made Jacob miserable, changing his wages several times, essentially keeping him as a slave. Finally, in the middle of the night, Jacob and his wives escape from Laban, with Laban chasing after them.

For this reason, Laban is considered one of the villains of the Bible. Here's how he comes off in the Passover Haggadah: "Go out and learn what Laban wanted to do to Jacob our father. Pharaoh wanted to kill only the boys, but Laban sought to destroy Jacob's entire family."

Why is there so much drama between Jacob and Laban? Perhaps because it serves as a sort of "coming attractions" for Jacob's descendants, who will be enslaved in Egypt. We can see Laban as an earlier version of Pharaoh. And the way that Jacob and his family left Laban—in the middle of the night, with Laban chasing them—is exactly the way that the Israelites would leave Egypt, generations later.

But there is more. Jacob had deceived his father, Isaac, by stealing the blessing reserved for his brother, Esau—and Jacob was able to do that because Isaac was blind. In exactly the same way, Laban took advantage of Jacob's "blindness" in the darkness of his wedding night, and he switched Leah for Rachel. The ancient Rabbis called this *middah k'neged middah*, "measure for measure." We would say: what goes around, comes around. It's all payback.

Or, maybe it's not just revenge, and not just payback. Maybe there's a purpose behind it all. Perhaps it's to teach Jacob a lesson—to make him a better person. In the words of Israeli statesman Avraham Burg: "Jacob is the ultimate proof of our claim that the entire Torah is, among other things, the improvement manual for our forefathers' character flaws. It's an improvement process that obligates each and every one of us, all day, every day. Happy is the person who is always improving."

## Connections

> Which interpretation of the identity of the angels on the stairway do you like the most? Why? Do you have any other interpretations?

> If you could imagine the angels of adulthood speaking to Jacob, what do you think they would say? What would your "angels" say to you?

> Do you agree with Jacob's fear to go up on the stairway? Why was he afraid to take the risk? What risks have you been willing, or unwilling, to take?

> Jacob's experience with Laban forced him to confront some of the flaws in his character. Everyone has flaws; which of your flaws or weaknesses do you want to work on? What are you particularly good at doing? How do you want to strengthen your skills and your positive points?

> What historical figures have had lives like Jacob—filled with ups and downs? Some examples: Abraham Lincoln, Franklin Roosevelt, Mother Teresa, Helen Keller, Oprah Winfrey. Do you have friends or family members who have had ups and downs? What lessons can you learn from their stories?goes on today. It is about people who don't take Judaism seriously, and kind of sleepwalk through the service. They lack *kavanah*—the ability to spiritually connect with what is going on.

# THE HAFTARAH

❖ Va-yetse': Hosea 12:13–14:10

Imagine yourself in a hot-air balloon, sailing across all of biblical history. That would be a good way of understanding this haftarah. The prophet Hosea lived in the Northern Kingdom of Israel, which was also called Ephraim (after one of Joseph's sons). Hosea reminds the People of Israel that Jacob fled back to Aram and guarded the sheep of his father-in-law, Laban (the link to the Torah portion). As a parallel, it was another prophet—Moses—who guarded the Jewish people on their way out of Egypt.

Hosea then takes us on a whirlwind tour: through the wilderness experience, when the Israelites worshiped the idol Baal and suffered a plague as punishment; through the people's desire for a king in the time of the prophet Samuel (Hosea 13:10–11)—all the way to the idolatrous, Baal-worshiping practices of the Northern Kingdom. When Hosea mentions how the Israelites died in the wilderness because they worshiped Baal, he means this as a warning to the Israelites of the Northern Kingdom, who were doing the same thing.

Hosea's words are stern, and yet he believes that it is both possible and necessary for the people of the Northern Kingdom to repent (in fact, part of this haftarah is also read on Shabbat Shuvah, the Shabbat of Repentance, which comes between Rosh Hashanah and Yom Kippur). Hosea concludes his words with the hope that the wise will consider his words and heed them.

## Human Life

Here's a question: You and your family are in the middle of a terrible storm. Your neighborhood is flooded, and you have a rowboat. You see your dog, Dexter. Then you also see your down-the-street neighbor Mr. Green. You only have room in your boat for one more passenger. You can save either your dog, Dexter, whom you love, or Mr. Green, whom you barely know. What do you do?

While you're thinking about that, let's go back to the haftarah. The prophet Hosea lived and preached in the Northern Kingdom of Israel. During his time many Israelites still worshiped the Canaanite god Baal in the form of an idol of a calf (this is similar to the sin of the Golden Calf, Exodus 32). Hosea criticizes his countrymen for "kissing calves" and adds a very strange statement: "they appoint men to sacrifice" (13:2). While the Hebrew is uncertain, some scholars see this as a reference (likely a warning) about human sacrifice that may have still been carried out by the neighboring Canaanites.

Hosea was horrified at the thought that any society could think about worshiping animals while sacrificing people. Awful.

Back to Dexter and Mr. Green and the raging flood waters. Whom are you going to save?

In a famous study, Professor Richard Topolski asked his students a similar question and discovered: "Everyone would save a sibling, grandparent or close friend rather than a strange dog. But when people considered their own dog versus people less connected with them—a distant cousin or a hometown stranger—votes in favor of saving the dog came rolling in!"

There you go: people who kiss calves (or, love their dogs) might, in a difficult situation, choose to save an animal over a human. It's not "Who do we love more—Dexter or Mr. Green?" Obviously, Dexter will win. But Dexter should not win. Mr. Green should win.

Judaism's point is: People are made in God's image, and animals (even though we love them) are not. And being made in God's image trumps everything else. Every human being is sacred in a way that animals are not. While animals are living beings, and Judaism has laws against cruelty to animals, let's remember that humans come first. Saving a human life, even at the expense of an animal's, is the greatest good. The Talmud teaches that when we save a human life we have saved an entire world.

So, save Mr. Green. It's the right thing to do.

❖ Notes

❖ Notes

Lightning Source UK Ltd.
Milton Keynes UK
UKHW012003300820
368968UK00014B/321

# THE JPS B'NAI MITZVAH TORAH COMMENTARY

**Va-yishlaḥ** (Genesis 32:4–36:43)
Haftarah (Obadiah 1:1–21)

Rabbi Jeffrey K. Salkin

The Jewish Publication Society · Philadelphia
University of Nebraska Press · Lincoln

# INTRODUCTION

News flash: the most important thing about becoming bar or bat mitzvah isn't the party. Nor is it the presents. Nor even being able to celebrate with your family and friends—as wonderful as those things are. Nor is it even standing before the congregation and reading the prayers of the liturgy—as important as that is.

No, the most important thing about becoming bar or bat mitzvah is sharing Torah with the congregation. And why is that? Because of all Jewish skills, that is the most important one.

Here is what is true about rites of passage: you can tell what a culture values by the tasks it asks its young people to perform on their way to maturity. In American culture, you become responsible for driving, responsible for voting, and yes, responsible for drinking responsibly.

In some cultures, the rite of passage toward maturity includes some kind of trial, or a test of strength. Sometimes, it is a kind of "outward bound" camping adventure. Among the Maasai tribe in Africa, it is traditional for a young person to hunt and kill a lion. In some Hispanic cultures, fifteen year-old girls celebrate the *quinceañera*, which marks their entrance into maturity.

What is Judaism's way of marking maturity? It combines both of these rites of passage: *responsibility* and *test*. You show that you are on your way to becoming a *responsible* Jewish adult through a public *test* of strength and knowledge—reading or chanting Torah, and then teaching it to the congregation.

This is the most important Jewish ritual mitzvah (commandment), and that is how you demonstrate that you are, truly, bar or bat mitzvah—old enough to be responsible for the mitzvot.

## What Is Torah?

So, what exactly is the Torah? You probably know this already, but let's review.

The Torah (teaching) consists of "the five books of Moses," sometimes also called the *chumash* (from the Hebrew word *chameish*, which means "five"), or, sometimes, the Greek word Pentateuch (which means "the five teachings").

Here are the five books of the Torah, with their common names and their Hebrew names.

> **Genesis (The beginning), which in Hebrew is Bere'shit (from the first words—"When God began to create").** Bere'shit spans the years from Creation to Joseph's death in Egypt. Many of the Bible's best stories are in Genesis: the creation story itself; Adam and Eve in the Garden of Eden; Cain and Abel; Noah and the Flood; and the tales of the Patriarchs and Matriarchs, Abraham, Isaac, Jacob, Sarah, Rebekah, Rachel, and Leah. It also includes one of the greatest pieces of world literature, the story of Joseph, which is actually the oldest complete novel in history, comprising more than one-quarter of all Genesis.

> **Exodus (Getting out), which in Hebrew is Shemot (These are the names).** Exodus begins with the story of the Israelite slavery in Egypt. It then moves to the rise of Moses as a leader, and the Israelites' liberation from slavery. After the Israelites leave Egypt, they experience the miracle of the parting of the Sea of Reeds (or "Red Sea"); the giving of the Ten Commandments at Mount Sinai; the idolatry of the Golden Calf; and the design and construction of the Tabernacle and of the ark for the original tablets of the law, which our ancestors carried with them in the desert. Exodus also includes various ethical and civil laws, such as "You shall not wrong a stranger or oppress him, for you were strangers in the land of Egypt" (22:20).

> **Leviticus (about the Levites), or, in Hebrew, Va-yikra' (And God called).** It goes into great detail about the kinds of sacrifices that the ancient Israelites brought as offerings; the laws of ritual purity; the animals that were permitted and forbidden for eating (the beginnings of the tradition of kashrut, the Jewish dietary laws); the diagnosis of various skin diseases; the ethical laws of holiness; the ritual calendar of the Jewish year; and various agricultural laws concerning the treatment of the Land of Israel. Leviticus is basically the manual of ancient Judaism.

> Numbers (because the book begins with the census of the Isra-elites), or, in Hebrew, Be-midbar (In the wilderness). The book describes the forty years of wandering in the wilderness and the various rebellions against Moses. The constant theme: "Egypt wasn't so bad. Maybe we should go back." The greatest rebellion against Moses was the negative reports of the spies about the Land of Israel, which discouraged the Israelites from wanting to move forward into the land. For that reason, the "wilderness generation" must die off before a new generation can come into maturity and finish the journey.

> Deuteronomy (The repetition of the laws of the Torah), or, in Hebrew, Devarim (The words). The final book of the Torah is, essentially, Moses's farewell address to the Israelites as they prepare to enter the Land of Israel. Here we find various laws that had been previously taught, though sometimes with different wording. Much of Deuteronomy contains laws that will be important to the Israelites as they enter the Land of Israel—laws concerning the establishment of a monarchy and the ethics of warfare. Perhaps the most famous passage from Deuteronomy contains the *Shema,* the declaration of God's unity and uniqueness, and the *Ve-ahavta,* which follows it. Deuteronomy ends with the death of Moses on Mount Nebo as he looks across the Jordan Valley into the land that he will not enter.

Jews read the Torah in sequence—starting with Bere'shit right after Simchat Torah in the autumn, and then finishing Devarim on the following Simchat Torah. Each Torah portion is called a parashah (division; sometimes called a *sidrah,* a place in the order of the Torah reading). The stories go around in a full circle, reminding us that we can always gain more insights and more wisdom from the Torah. This means that if you don't "get" the meaning this year, don't worry—it will come around again.

## And What Else? The Haftarah

We read or chant the Torah from the Torah scroll—the most sacred thing that a Jewish community has in its possession. The Torah is written without vowels, and the ability to read it and chant it is part of the challenge and the test.

But there is more to the synagogue reading. Every Torah reading has an accompanying haftarah reading. Haftarah means "conclusion," because there was once a time when the service actually ended with that reading. Some scholars believe that the reading of the haftarah originated at a time when non-Jewish authorities outlawed the reading of the Torah, and the Jews read the haftarah sections instead. In fact, in some synagogues, young people who become bar or bat mitzvah read very little Torah and instead read the entire haftarah portion.

The haftarah portion comes from the Nevi'im, the prophetic books, which are the second part of the Jewish Bible. It is either read or chanted from a Hebrew Bible, or maybe from a booklet or a photocopy.

The ancient sages chose the haftarah passages because their themes reminded them of the words or stories in the Torah text. Sometimes, they chose *haftarah* with special themes in honor of a festival or an upcoming festival.

Not all books in the prophetic section of the Hebrew Bible consist of prophecy. Several are historical. For example:

The book of Joshua tells the story of the conquest and settlement of Israel.

The book of Judges speaks of the period of early tribal rulers who would rise to power, usually for the purpose of uniting the tribes in war against their enemies. Some of these leaders are famous: Deborah, the great prophetess and military leader, and Samson, the biblical strong man.

The books of Samuel start with Samuel, the last judge, and then move to the creation of the Israelite monarchy under Saul and David (approximately 1000 BCE).

The books of Kings tell of the death of King David, the rise of King Solomon, and how the Israelite kingdom split into the Northern Kingdom of Israel and the Southern Kingdom of Judah (approximately 900 BCE).

And then there are the books of the prophets, those spokesmen for God whose words fired the Jewish conscience. Their names are immortal: Isaiah, Jeremiah, Ezekiel, Amos, Hosea, among others.

Someone once said: "There is no evidence of a biblical prophet ever being invited back a second time for dinner." Why? Because the prophets were tough. They had no patience for injustice, apathy, or hypocrisy. No one escaped their criticisms. Here's what they taught:

> ➤ God commands the Jews to behave decently toward one another. In fact, God cares more about basic ethics and decency than about ritual behavior.
> ➤ God chose the Jews *not* for special privileges, but for special duties to humanity.
> ➤ As bad as the Jews sometimes were, there was always the possibility that they would improve their behavior.
> ➤ As bad as things might be now, it will not always be that way. Someday, there will be universal justice and peace. Human history is moving forward toward an ultimate conclusion that some call the Messianic Age: a time of universal peace and prosperity for the Jewish people and for all the people of the world.

## Your Mission—To Teach Torah to the Congregation

On the day when you become bar or bat mitzvah, you will be reading, or chanting, Torah—in Hebrew. You will be reading, or chanting, the haftarah—in Hebrew. That is the major skill that publicly marks the becoming of bar or bat mitzvah. But, perhaps even more important than that, you need to be able to teach something about the Torah portion, and perhaps the haftarah as well.

And that is where this book comes in. It will be a very valuable resource for you, and your family, in the b'nai mitzvah process.

Here is what you will find in it:

> ➤ A brief **summary** of every Torah portion. This is a basic overview of the portion; and, while it might not refer to everything in the Torah portion, it will explain its most important aspects.
> ➤ A list of the **major ideas** in the Torah portion. The purpose: to make the Torah portion real, in ways that we can relate to. Every Torah portion contains unique ideas, and when you put all

of those ideas together, you actually come up with a list of Judaism's most important ideas.

> Two **divrei Torah** ("words of Torah," or "sermonettes") for each portion. These *divrei Torah* explain significant aspects of the Torah portion in accessible, reader-friendly language. Each *devar Torah* contains references to **traditional** Jewish sources (those that were written before the modern era), as well as **modern** sources and quotes. We have searched, far and wide, to find sources that are unusual, interesting, and not just the "same old stuff" that many people already know about the Torah portion. Why did we include these minisermons in the volume? Not because we want you to simply copy those sermons and pass them off as your own (that would be cheating), though you are free to quote from them. We included them so that you can see what is possible— how you can try to make meaning for yourself out of the words of Torah.

> **Connections:** This is perhaps the most valuable part. It's a list of questions that you can ask yourself, or that others might help you think about—any of which can lead to the creation of your *devar Torah.*

Note: you don't have to like everything that's in a particular Torah portion. Some aren't that loveable. Some are hard to understand; some are about religious practices that people today might find confusing, and even offensive; some contain ideas that we might find totally outmoded.

But this doesn't have to get in the way. After all, most kids spend a lot of time thinking about stories that contain ideas that modern people would find totally bizarre. Any good medieval fantasy story falls into that category.

And we also believe that, if you spend just a little bit of time with those texts, you can begin to understand what the author was trying to say.

This volume goes one step further. Sometimes, the haftarah comes off as a second thought, and no one really thinks about it. We have tried to solve that problem by including a **summary** of each haftarah, and then a mini-sermon on the haftarah. This will help you learn how these sacred words are relevant to today's world, and even to your own life.

All Bible quotations come from the NJPS translation, which is found in the many different editions of the JPS TANAKH; in the Conservative movement's *Etz Hayim: Torah and Commentary;* in the Reform movement's *Torah: A Modern Commentary;* and in other Bible commentaries and study guides.

### How Do I Write a *Devar Torah?*

It really is easier than it looks.

There are many ways of thinking about the *devar Torah*. It is, of course, a short sermon on the meaning of the Torah (and, perhaps, the haftarah) portion. It might even be helpful to think of the *devar Torah* as a "book report" on the portion itself.

The most important thing you can know about this sacred task is: *Learn* the words. *Love* the words. Teach people what it could mean to *live* the words.

Here's a basic outline for a *devar Torah:*

"My Torah portion is (name of portion) _____,
    from the book of _____, chapter

    _____.

"In my Torah portion, we learn that_____
    (Summary of portion)
"For me, the most important lesson of this Torah portion is (what
    is the best thing in the portion? Take the portion as a whole;
    your *devar Torah* does not have to be only, or specifically, on the
    verses that you are reading).
"As I learned my Torah portion, I found myself wondering:
    ‣ *Raise a question that the Torah portion itself raises.*
    ‣ *"Pick a fight"* with the portion. Argue with it.
    ‣ *Answer a question* that is listed in the "Connections" section of
        each Torah portion.
    ‣ *Suggest a question to your rabbi* that you would want the rabbi
        to answer in his or her own *devar Torah* or sermon.

"I have lived the values of the Torah by _____
(here, you can talk about how the Torah portion relates to your
own life. If you have done a mitzvah project, you can talk about
that here).

## How To Keep It from Being Boring
## (and You from Being Bored)

Some people just don't like giving traditional speeches. From our perspective, that's really okay. Perhaps you can teach Torah in a different
way—one that makes sense to you.

> Write an "open letter" to one of the characters in your Torah por-
  tion. "Dear Abraham: I hope that your trip to Canaan was not too
  hard . . ." "Dear Moses: Were you afraid when you got the Ten
  Commandments on Mount Sinai? I sure would have been . . ."
> Write a news story about what happens. Imagine yourself to
  be a television or news reporter. "Residents of neighboring cities were horrified yesterday as the wicked cities of Sodom and
  Gomorrah were burned to the ground. Some say that God was
  responsible . . ."
> Write an imaginary interview with a character in your Torah portion.
> Tell the story from the point of view of another character, or a mi-
  nor character, in the story. For instance, tell the story of the Garden of Eden from the point of view of the serpent. Or the story
  of the Binding of Isaac from the point of view of the ram, which
  was substituted for Isaac as a sacrifice. Or perhaps the story of
  the sale of Joseph from the point of view of his coat, which was
  stripped off him and dipped in a goat's blood.
> Write a poem about your Torah portion.
> Write a song about your Torah portion.
> Write a play about your Torah portion, and have some friends act
  it out with you.
> Create a piece of artwork about your Torah portion.

The bottom line is: Make this a joyful experience. Yes—it could
even be fun.

### The Very Last Thing You Need to Know at This Point

The Torah scroll is written without vowels. Why? Don't *sofrim* (Torah scribes) know the vowels?

Of course they do.

So, why do they leave the vowels out?

One reason is that the Torah came into existence at a time when sages were still arguing about the proper vowels, and the proper pronunciation.

But here is another reason: The Torah text, as we have it today, and as it sits in the scroll, is actually *an unfinished work*. Think of it: the words are just sitting there. Because they have no vowels, it is as if they have no voice.

When we read the Torah publicly, we give voice to the ancient words. And when we find meaning in those ancient words, and we talk about those meanings, those words jump to life. They enter our lives. They make our world deeper and better.

Mazal tov to you, and your family. This is your journey toward Jewish maturity. Love it.

# THE TORAH

❖ Va-yishlaḥ: Genesis 32:4–36:43

Jacob realizes that he has a piece of unfinished business to take care of.
He has to finally face up to his brother, Esau, and he's afraid that Esau
might kill him. The reunion comes off better than Jacob had expected.

But Jacob's troubles are far from over. He winds up wounded from
an all-night wrestling match with a mysterious, nameless stranger,
and that leaves him with a limp for the rest of his life. And then his
daughter, Dinah, gets raped by a Canaanite prince. To top it off, his
beloved wife, Rachel, dies in childbirth. It can't get worse. But, of
course, it does—and it will.

### Summary

> ‣ Jacob brings his family, his animals, and gifts to his brother, Esau. (32:4–22)
> ‣ The night before their meeting, Jacob wrestled with a mysterious stranger, who changed his name to Israel. (Gen 32:23–33)
> ‣ Jacob's fears about his reunion with Esau dissolve when Esau greets him lovingly, and they tearfully reunite. (33:1–17)
> ‣ Jacob's daughter, Dinah, is raped by a Canaanite prince, and her brothers viciously retaliate against the city of Shechem, the place where it happened. (34:1–31)
> ‣ Rachel dies while giving birth to her son Benjamin, and Jacob buries her on the road to Ephrath (now Bethlehem) and builds a pillar over her grave. (35:16–21)
> ‣ The descendants of Esau are listed. (36:1–43)

## The Big Ideas

> **Judaism means wrestling**—with the world, with God, and with yourself. Judaism does not believe that life should be easy; rather, our challenges can be useful to us. That value is found in the very name of the Jewish people—*Yisrael,* which is often translated as "the one who wrestles with God."

> **Wounds are important.** Most people get "wounded" in life somehow, and our wounds can become ways to grow.

> **Facing your failings is crucial for moral growth.** It can be very scary to face people whom you have hurt. But when you do, it can be better than you imagined. You can also grow from the experience.

> **Serious divisions in families need not be forever.** Jacob and Esau eventually put their differences aside and make up with each other. Crises in families can be healed if people make honest efforts to do so.

> **Extreme violence, even in self-defense, is inappropriate.** While we can understand that Dinah's brothers were furious that she had been raped, their extremely violent act of revenge is simply over-the-top awful. Jacob believes that their actions have brought disrepute to his family, and years later he curses Levi and Simeon for their actions (34:30).

> **It takes more than Jews to create the Jewish story.** Even though the descendants of Esau are not Jewish, they (and he) are important enough to merit an entire chapter of the Torah (chapter 36). Moreover, the Torah goes out of its way to mention that the Edomites, the descendants of Esau, had kings even before there were any kings in Israel (36:31)—as if to remind the ancient Israelites that they were not the first in the "king department," and to keep them humble.

*Divrei Torah*

MEETING ESAU AND MAKING WAR

It has been many years since Jacob cheated his brother, Esau—out of his birthright and out of his blessing as the firstborn. Ever since then, Jacob has learned about life the hard way. He fled to his family's homeland in Aram-naharaim, and there his uncle Laban deceived him, giving him Leah as a wife instead of Rachel, for whom he will work an additional seven years. In the ensuing years, Jacob has a family. He becomes rich in flocks and herds. And then comes the moment when he knows that the unfinished business of his life has caught up with him. Jacob is about to reunite with Esau. He knows that he must make peace with him, and he is frightened.

Perhaps that explains why Jacob constantly refers to himself as a "servant." And he keeps referring to Esau as "my lord." Having once dreamed of angels climbing a ladder, it is as if he has suddenly discovered humility. More than that: as he is preparing to meet Esau, he sends him gifts, hoping that he can gain his favor. That's Jacob. He is always practical. He is either taking gifts, such as the birthright from Esau and the blessing from his father, Isaac; or he is giving gifts—now to Esau and later to his son Joseph.

But what is making Jacob really nervous as he prepares to have a reunion with his brother, Esau? The text says: "Jacob was greatly frightened; in his anxiety, he divided the people with him" (32:8). In the words of the great medieval commentator Rashi: "He was afraid that he might be killed, and he was afraid that he would have to kill."

Judaism says that if you have to fight a war, do it—but only if it is absolutely necessary. If you have to use force, only use the amount of force that is absolutely necessary. Soldiers should avoid targeting civilians as much as is humanly possible.

This is especially true of Israel. Former prime minister of Israel Golda Meir was rumored to have said: "We can forgive the Arabs for killing our children. We cannot forgive them for forcing us to kill their children. We will only have peace with the Arabs when they love their children more than they hate us."

War stinks. If you have to, fight. But don't enjoy it.

WHO WAS THAT MAN?

Jacob's night wrestling is one of the most famous episodes in the entire Torah, and in all literature.

Jacob, on the eve of his reunion with his brother, Esau, who has previously sworn to kill him, sends his family ahead of him across the Jabbok River. (Interesting thing about the Jabbok River: its name is actually a mixed-up way of saying Jacob's name. There's a pun there, as well. In Hebrew, Jabbok sounds like the word *evek,* "wrestling"— which is exactly what Jacob is about to do.)

There, Jacob was left alone, "And a man wrestled with him until the break of dawn" (32:25). Why is this wrestling match happening? We don't know. We have no sense of motives here. Why was Jacob attacked? We don't know.

Who is the wrestling partner? That is something else we don't know. But the possibilities teach us a lot about Judaism, and about ourselves.

The Torah says that it is a man. Was it simply a stranger? Perhaps Jacob's brother, Esau?

Maybe it was a more mysterious being, an angel of some sort. The ancient Rabbis say that "it was the guardian Prince of Esau." In Jewish lore, Esau is the ancestor of all enemies of the Jews. So, the guardian Prince of Esau is the spirit of all those who have wanted to destroy the Jews—sort of like an eternal Darth Vader. At that moment, Jacob started a wrestling match with the forces of evil, and that wrestling match has continued, unbroken, to our own time.

Was Jacob wrestling with God? That's certainly how the tradition understands it; his name becomes Israel, the one who struggled with God. This is huge. To wrestle with God can mean, to some people, wondering whether God really exists, or wondering why God allows certain things to happen. It can also mean wrestling with what our relationship with God should be, with what God wants of us.

Perhaps Jacob was wrestling with himself—the part of himself with big conflicts about all the less-than-wonderful things he has done in his life, like stealing a birthright and a blessing. The "stranger" has to ask Jacob his name because he wants to know if Jacob is going to own up to who he really is. Rabbi Shmuel Klitsner writes: "This night-time being functions as Jacob's own dark side. At the same time, the stranger functions as the divine image within Jacob. If Jacob can be whole, it is by struggling with the human and the divine within himself." Jacob limps away from that all-night wrestling match.

Sometimes, looking at ourselves realistically and critically can hurt. It takes courage to do it. But it is necessary.

## Connections

- What have you struggled with? A bad habit, perhaps? Have you made progress?
- In what ways could you say you struggle with God?
- In what ways do we struggle with ourselves?
- The midrash says that Jacob wrestled with the Prince of Esau, which means that he wrestled with all of the Jews' enemies throughout history. Who are some of those enemies? How have Jacob's descendants—the Jewish people—struggled against them?
- Have you ever reconciled with someone with whom you had a real disagreement or a deep conflict? What was it like?Judaism's point is: People are made in God's image, and animals (even though we love them) are not. And being made in God's image trumps everything else. Every human being is sacred in a way that animals are not. While animals are living beings, and Judaism has laws against cruelty to animals, let's remember that humans come first. Saving a human life, even at the expense of an animal's, is the greatest good. The Talmud teaches that when we save a human life we have saved an entire world.

So, save Mr. Green. It's the right thing to do.

# THE HAFTARAH

## ❖ Va-yishlaḥ: Obadiah 1:1–21

The prophet Obadiah was a "downer." Everything he said was bleak. The whole book is only one chapter long—the shortest book in the Bible—and it is a denunciation of the ancient nation of Edom, which helped the Babylonians destroy the ancient kingdom of Judea.

As we know, in the Torah portion Jacob and his brother, Esau, are about to be reunited. Remember that Esau had sold his birthright to Jacob. Esau's other name is Edom, which means "red"—both because his complexion and hair were red, and because of the red-colored soup that he bought from Jacob in exchange for the birthright. Esau = Edom.

The kingdom of Edom is descended from Esau. And the kingdom of Judea is descended from Jacob; it's named after Judah, one of his sons. So Obadiah sees the struggle between the ancient Judeans and the kingdom of Edom as a continuation of the struggle between Jacob and Esau.

Every prophetic book of the Bible ends on a note of hope, except Obadiah. This prophet trashes the nation of Edom, and the haftarah (and the book of Obadiah itself) ends with the prophet teaching that Edom will ultimately be defeated. A real downer.

### What Ever Happened to Brotherly Love?

The prophet Obadiah is totally angry about what Edom did to Israel. You might be too if you had to deal with an enemy who had helped destroy your country!

It was bad enough that the Edomites (descendants of Esau) helped the enemies of the Jews. But think about this—it was like turning on your family—because they helped defeat the Judeans, who were their distant cousins! True, Jacob and Esau were not exactly close; neither were their descendants. When Jacob cheated Esau out of the blessing that was reserved for him as the oldest son, Esau threatened to kill him. But years later—and in the Torah portion—Jacob and Esau meet again. We cannot say that they totally made up with each other.

Each went their separate way. Jacob mumbled something about visiting Esau in Seir, Esau's territory—but he never did. Okay, maybe there were still some lingering bad feelings, but they put an end to their years of alienation.

Obadiah is disappointed. He hoped for better from the descendants of Esau. True—sometimes families have tensions, and sometimes family members don't talk. But, please, you simply don't help in their destruction.

But there may be another intriguing reason why Obadiah is so angry, and it's *personal*.

According to the ancient Rabbis, Obadiah had originally been an Edomite before he became a Jew: "Obadiah was an Edomite who joined the Jewish people." If this is true, then his own people had disappointed him. It is as if his birth family turned on his adopted family, all of whom are related.

No wonder Obadiah is so angry!

Obadiah's rant is a warning that even family can disappoint. But if we remember where we all come from, and how we are connected, then like Jacob and Esau, regaining brotherly love is always possible, if not probable.

❖ Notes

❖ Notes